Easy Olympic

Gymnastics

10 9 8 7 6 5 4 3 2 1

ISBN   1-58000-112-2
TCM   6135

DIR./OPERATIONS . . . . .Robin L. Howland
PROJECT MANAGER . . . . .Bryan K. Howland
AUTHOR .Debra J. Housel, M.S. Ed.
EDITOR . . . . .Eric Migliaccio
DESIGNER . . . . .Phil Garcia
PHOTOGRAPHS . . . . .Getty Images
COVER PHOTOS . . . . .Mike Powell

                              Published in association with
                              and distributed by:

Griffin Publishing Group   **Teacher Created Materials**
18022 Cowan, Suite 202   6421 Industry Way
Irvine, CA 92614   Westminster, CA 92683
www.griffinpublishing.com   www.teachercreated.com

Manufactured in the United States of America

Gymnastics is an Olympic sport.

Gymnasts move their bodies in special ways.

3

Gymnasts must be strong.

They need good
balance.

All gymnasts do flips
and jumps.

Sometimes they do them on the beam.

Sometimes they do them in the air.

CLIVE BRUNSKILL

They learn to fly from one bar to another.

They do cartwheels and splits.

They run to a springboard and jump.

DOUG PENSINGER

They must land on their feet.

Male gymnasts do tricks on the rings.

They swing on the
pommel horse.

They pull themselves
up and over a bar.

The best gymnasts win medals.